1994 Edition
Published by Wishing Well Books,
an imprint of Joshua Morris Publishing, Inc.,
221 Danbury Road, Wilton, CT 06897.
ISBN: 0-88705-751-9
10 9 8 7 6 5 4 3 2 1

Look Out for Rosy!

BOB GRAHAM

WISHING WELL BOOKS

Rosy hears a "click" at the front gate.
She uses her ears.

She listens to the sound from the gate.
It is Mike coming home.

Rosy sees Mike.
She uses her eyes.

She is happy to see him.
Watch out, Mike!

Rosy flies through the air.
She wants to say hello to Mike.

The ice cream is cold.
Mike feels it on his skin.

Down goes Mike!

The ice cream flies
high in the air.

Mike has scraped his elbow
and his knee. His skin hurts.

Rosy is not hurt at all.

But what's this? Rosy is
smelling Mike's ice cream.

She uses her nose.
The ice cream smells good.

Too late, Mike! Rosy is tasting
the ice cream.

She uses her tongue.
The ice cream tastes good too!

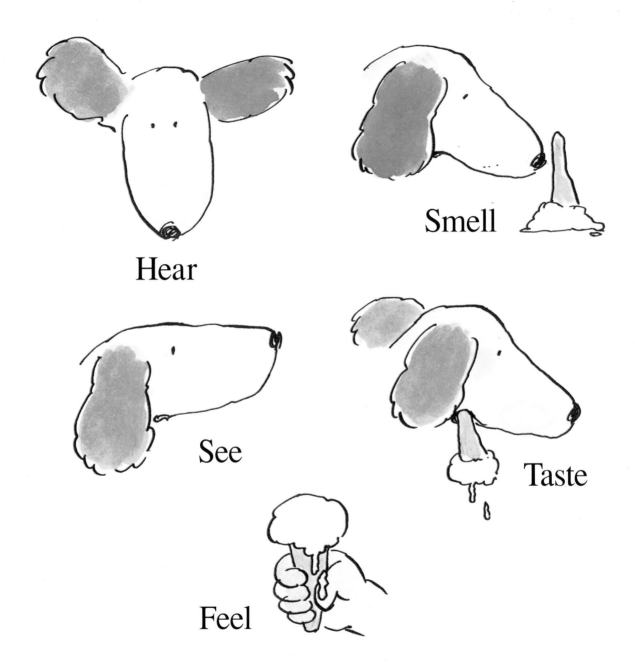

Hear

Smell

See

Taste

Feel

senses

Senses are the means by which we receive information about what is happening in our environment. The senses provide information about things either away from the body or in contact with the body. The senses of hearing and sight are called distance-receiving senses; they respond to traveling waves of sound and light, respectively. The senses of taste, touch, and smell respond to things that come in contact with the body.

Experiments to try

1. Ask your child to distinguish between the taste of an apple and a potato. Have your child taste each with eyes closed and then with nose blocked. Is it more difficult to distinguish taste in either of these cases?

2. Whisper something very softly to your child. Can your voice be heard? Try saying the same thing, a little louder each time, until your child can repeat what you say.

3. Line up a variety of objects—some with smooth surfaces, some with rough surfaces, some cold or hot, and so on. Ask your child to feel each object and describe the differences between them.

4. Fill plastic containers of the same size with three different items, such as rice, marbles, and raisins. Shake each container in turn, and have your child try to guess by sound which substance is in each container.